Living Shrines

Shrine to the Virgin, Los Ojos

LIVING SHRINES

Home Altars of New Mexico

TEXT BY MARIE ROMERO CASH

PHOTOGRAPHS BY SIEGFRIED HALUS

ESSAY BY LUCY R. LIPPARD

MUSEUM OF NEW MEXICO PRESS
SANTA FE

Copyright © 1998 Museum of New Mexico Press. Text by Marie Romero Cash © the author; photographs by Siegfried Halus © the photographer. *All rights reserved.* No part of this book may be reproduced in any part or by any means whatsoever with the exception of brief passages embodied in critical reviews without the express written consent of the publisher.

Project editor: Mary Wachs
Design and production: David Skolkin
Assistant designer: Susan Surprise
Set in New Caledonia and Caslon Open Face
Manufactured in Hong Kong
10 9 8 7 6 5 4 3 2 1

Library of Congress Cataloging-in-Publication Data

Cash, Marie Romero.
    Living Shrines : home altars of New Mexico / by Marie Romero
Cash ; photographs by Siegfried Halus ; essay by Lucy R. Lippard.
        p.   cm.
    Includes bibliographical references.
    ISBN 0-89013-369-7. — ISBN 0-89013-370-0 (pbk.)
    1. Household shrines—New Mexico. 2. New Mexico—Religious
life and customs. I. Lippard, Lucy R. II. Title.
BL2527.N6C37   1998
246—dc21   96-26816
                                                                CIP

MUSEUM OF NEW MEXICO PRESS
Post Office Box 2087
Santa Fe, New Mexico 87504

Contents

Eliza Mondragon's personal shrine, Ranchos de Taos

Acknowledgments

Marie Romero Cash and I are grateful to all those who so graciously opened their homes and hearts to us as we traveled throughout Northern New Mexico. These testaments helped to enlarge our knowledge of what moves people to perpetuate these acts of devotion that involve the creation and maintenance of their shrines. While listening to personal tales, histories, and insights, we felt blessed by their clarity and genuineness. Under these warm and embracing circumstances, much was discovered, the breadth of which we hope is transmitted in this book.

We wish to thank Lucy Lippard for her marvelous text. Her contributions extend the field of discourse about shrines. We also wish to thank Mary Wachs, editorial director, and David Skolkin, art director, Museum of New Mexico Press. A special thanks to Kathy King for her support of the photographic portion of this project; and to Mr. and Mrs. Emilio Romero, whose devotional space was the inspiration for this book.

As the photographer, I felt doubly blessed by what I had gained in our experiences reflecting the heightened importance of the documentation of these shrines, as though these individuals felt themselves intrinsically a part of this quest, this notion of definition. It is our hope that upon seeing the images of their shrines in this book, these participants will recall those shared moments in which our lives intersected; and *that* in itself is the best acknowledgment.

— SIEGFRIED HALUS

Introduction

MARIE ROMERO CASH

My introduction to home altars came about during my childhood. My mother, Senaida Romero, always kept a makeshift altar of sorts on top of one of the dressers in the living room. This altar served to hold the statues of the Sacred Heart, Blessed Virgin Mary, and St. Anthony, to which we prayed each night before going to bed. In 1949, when I was seven years old, I earned the statue of the Blessed Virgin, a prize for attending mass every day during May, a contest held by the nuns at the Catholic school that each of us seven children was required to attend for two years until we made our First Communion. In addition, during May, we were required to kneel before our home altar each evening after dinner in order to pray the rosary. This went on until our late teens.

It was during this period in the late 1950s that I recall our home altar to have migrated to its space on top of an old record player that had been painted with flowers by an Anglo artist, Fern-Rae, with whom my tinsmith parents had collaborated. (They created tin frames for her contemporary renderings of various saints, along with making mirror frames incorporating her painted glass panels.) This was not the only devotional space in the house. As time wore on and we left the home to pursue our respective lives, *nichos* popped up all over the house, or perhaps I never noticed them as I grew up. Later, as my parents became more affluent tinsmiths, their main altar became more ornate. The blessed Santo Niño de Praga, a large statue of the Infant of Prague that had been given to them by the local order of Carmelite nuns, was enclosed in a glassed tin frame designed and made by my father, Emilio. (For many years the Carmelites would dress these figures in hand-sewn silk-and-satin robes to which they added sparkling sequins and beads.)

My own home altar did not begin to emerge until around the early 1980s, after my children began to leave the nest one by one. This began gradually at first—just a few statues on a small table. Then as my life prospered, I used a larger table, and then the present one, which has remained for about ten years.

The concept of writing a book about devotional spaces came to me while I was standing in front of my own home altar. When my brother, Bobby, passed away in November of 1997, my altar was significantly altered by this event. I placed a photograph of his smiling face

Emilio and Senaida Romero family shrine, Santa Fe

Marie Romero Cash, personal shrine, Santa Fe

on the altar, to which were attached two dried roses from his service. At the present time, this is the focus of my altar. I wanted to find other altars, to talk to the women and men who created them, who kept them up, about what had happened in their lives to make their altars a necessary part of their lives. Siegfried Halus and I began working together in spring 1996, traveling across Northern New Mexico seeking devotional shrines and an understanding of the motivation behind them. The interviews that follow represent a small portion of the riches uncovered in the long months of our collaboration.

The Garcia home in northeastern Santa Fe contains many items of devotion. Virginia Garcia has many stories concerning each of the pieces in her devotional space in the downstairs area of their home. As she talks about the antique piece in the center, she states:

> This little old lady sold my husband this, and it was on the
> day of my birthday, and oh, it was the greatest gift. It's the
> "holy altar call," that's what she called it. And it comes with
> a patent and they used to use it when they used to go to visit
> the sick people. And the strangest thing is, I'm very involved
> with the sick and the dying and when I received that, it meant
> so much to me. Another little treasure that I felt was God-sent
> was when a man came to my home, his name was Bo. He
> came one day with Our Lady of Guadalupe, and she's very

old because she's got long hair. I didn't react to it immediately and he left her with me. When he came to pick her up, I still didn't react. But when I went to push her hair back, and because I'm a beautician, I felt something between myself and the statue, and I didn't let him take it back.

She continues:

On one occasion I was visiting a sick person; there was a little girl there who I could tell really wanted to pray for the

Virginia Garcia family shrine, Santa Fe

sick lady. I had a rosary with me, and it was very special,
but I gave it to her anyway. I could tell it really meant some-
thing to her. Some days later, another lady brought me this
big rosary, and she was surprised to hear that I had recently
given mine away.

Both she and her sister Mary Lou have altars. They have traveled to various miracle sites together. As they were walking toward one site, a nun asked them their names. "Mary Lou and Maria Luisa," they replied, and she said, "Isn't it nice that as sisters you have the same names, one in English and one in Spanish." This was a fact that had never been pointed out to them.

Anita Thomas displays her Guadalupe on the fireplace ledge in a *nicho* made by her nephew, John Michael:

During World War II, my husband and I were stationed in
Bisbee, Arizona. One day we traveled to Nogales, Mexico,
and walked into a shop where I saw the most exquisite
statue of Our Lady of Guadalupe. I told my husband I was
going to buy it on the way out, so we wouldn't have to carry
it around all day. By the time we remembered, we were
already on our way home. I kept talking about it for days,
unable to get it off my mind. Some weeks later, my husband
took off from work, changed into civilian clothes, and

crossed the border into a town called Naco. There he found a Lady of Guadalupe, not as fine as the one I had originally picked out but beautiful nonetheless. For the past number of years because of illness my husband was bedridden. This beautiful lady kept him company.

Mrs. Julia Silva attributes several miracles to her Santo Niño. One of them is bringing back her sons safely when they served in the army in Vietnam, Puerto Rico, and other places. Another is that the house she now lives in and raised her family in was brought to her by praying to this Niño:

One morning in the early 1950s I found out that this house we wanted had been sold to another couple, and as I watched them moving in the furniture I began to cry, surrounded by my five then-small children. All day I felt badly, and then the seller of the house, Mrs. Pomonis, came to my door and told me, "Julia, I guess you are going to have the house after all." Shocked and surprised I asked, "What do you mean? I saw them moving in." Mrs. Pomonis related to me that Mr. Pomonis had gotten into an argument with them and that the deal was off. We then moved into the house of our dreams and my husband built a special nicho covered with pieces of mirror for the Santo Niño with the

7

crystal eyes. I come from a very spiritual family. I remember growing up in Santa Fe and my mother was a member of the Sacred Heart Society. The niño has many different robes, one for each season, ranging in color from white, red, green, and blue. I keep an album of prayers to the niño, and mostly as a reminder to help her remember them.

In the home of Lupe and Florence Sanchez, standing before their *nicho* dedicated to Our Lady of Guadalupe, Mrs. Sanchez recalls:

This nicho *is over fifty years old. My husband's mother had thrown it outside during remodeling. My husband went and got it and dug out a hole in my wall to put it in. Did you notice her nose? That's Lupe. Every night he prays to her and he touches her and he's rubbed away the paint! They used to do the same thing to the feet of the crucifix at the cathedral.*

Ray Herrera's outdoor shrine to the patron saint of Santa Fe, La Conquistadora, sits on a hill next to the Herrera home on Hillside Street above Santa Fe. He built the shrine some fifteen years ago, spurred on primarily by his devotion to this statue brought to Santa Fe by the first settlers, many of whom are his ancestors. At the entry to his workshop,

Julia Silva, Santo Niño shrine, Santa Fe

Lupe and Florence Sanchez, shrine to Our Lady of
Guadalupe, Santa Fe

he stops to light a candle to Our Lady of Guadalupe and say a prayer for whomever happens to be in need that day.

When Sara Armijo's outdoor shrine to the Blessed Virgin Mary is lit up at night during the Christmas season, everyone going up Apodaca Hill on Santa Fe's east side stops for a moment to take in the beauty of this stone monument and the statue that serenely gazes back. This is a peaceful place. Sara's devotion to the saints takes up most of her time. In addition to the grotto outside, she has four small altars inside of vary-

Ray Herrera, outdoor shrine, Santa Fe

Sara Armijo, Santa Fe

ing sizes. Each one has a special meaning to this very religious lady who spends most of her time praying for the needs of others. She has traveled to many countries and enjoys praying before those religious sites as she does in Santa Fe. She attributes many miracles to her Santo Niño and says her prayers are always answered. She places a piece of paper (on which the petition has been written) in the hand of the niño. When the request has been granted, she removes the paper and places it in the manila envelope below the altar, which is overflowing with petitions.

The drive into the town of El Rito is profuse with blossoms heralding the onset of spring. A few miles from the center of this sleepy community is the home of Nicolas Herrera and his mother, Celia. She is a slight woman, filled with enchanting stories of her childhood, including when her grandma was a moonshiner. She weaves a fascinating web as we sit and listen intently, almost forgetting our purpose for being there. The cozy fire in the wood stove beckons us to get comfortable and the simmering pots of posole and chile draw us in further. Celia tells us about her strong faith in the saints and the purpose of her home altar, which serves not only as a reminder of her personal devotion but also as a place to begin and end each day. As we walk through the house, there is a framed print of San Ramon with a quarter taped over his mouth. She explains:

> *He's the patron saint of attorneys and jails—and when there's going to be a lawsuit or a court hearing, I put a quar-*

ter on his mouth and tell him, "this quarter is going to stay on your mouth until the case is settled—so this is yours." As long as it takes, the quarter is there for the truth to come out, whether it's good or bad. The same is essentially true for San Calletano. You say, "I'll bet you two rosaries that you don't get me out of this mess." And San Martin dissipates gossip, sweeps the sins, and steps on snakes, the bad people.

Nicolas, whose great great-grandfather, José Inez Herrera, was a santero, also is following in his footsteps. He believes devoutly in Our Lady of Guadalupe simply because since he was a child his mother told him to. As a youngster, she dressed him, knelt in front of the altar at the Capilla de San Antonio, and said to the Virgin, "He's yours."

Their home altar is composed of various saints to which they both pray each morning and evening. Some of Nicolas's early carvings sit on the altar, and every time he travels, he brings something for his mother to put on the altar.

Driving toward Peñasco, a village situated deep in a national forest, we came upon the old convent that for many years had been the home for a group of nuns who taught school in the area. As we approached, we wondered if anyone was there who perhaps could direct us to people who might have altars in their homes. To our surprise, we ran into Joyce Kilgore, a woman who spent most of her days working for the church and school in Peñasco and the surrounding area. She led us to a small

Nicolas Herrera and his mother, Celia, El Rito

Old convent shrine, Peñasco

room at the back of the convent, whose walls were painted with angels. In the corner on top of a table was a makeshift altar with a number of saints surrounded by candles.

As we walked out into the snow-covered field in the backyard of the convent, we were greeted by a striking scene. There in the snow was a statue of the Virgin Mary surrounded by an arch of bright red plastic roses. The Virgin was bought by a Peñasco family whose daughter had been killed in an accident. Area teenagers hauled rocks from the riverbed to build the altar and shrine as a tribute to all youngsters who had died as a result of drunken drivers.

As we headed toward Villanueva, a community some forty miles from Santa Fe, we stopped at the small village of Bernal. At the church of Santa Rita, we found several grottos in the cemetery adjoining the church. Continuing along the highway, we came upon the village of Tecolote, a tiny farming community. As we scanned the area for shrines, we were drawn to the local cemetery. This is an area profuse with stonework, rock, and flagstone. We encountered several cemetery shrines, and as we walked toward the ancient burial site adjoining the cemetery, we saw beautifully primitive hand-carved headstones.

Some miles later we realized we had passed Villanueva, our original destination, by some twenty miles. As we backtracked, we marveled at the villages that seemed to be desperately holding on to their tradition and culture in the wake of paved roads and other incursions.

Throughout the area we discovered devotional shrines. Some we stumbled onto, and others we searched out in the hillside caves.

At Bernadette Vigil's home south of Santa Fe, we listened as the well-known painter explained the origins of her various altars. Bernadette has worked with gang members in Albuquerque to develop mural projects:

> It is very rewarding in that sometimes a career choice is made by a youngster who otherwise wouldn't have been exposed to art. It fills my heart to see the sparks that are ignited when a young person finds a talent in himself which he didn't know existed.

Bernadette Vigil, studio shrine

As we talk about her altars, we are drawn to a small green box on top of the refrigerator, which houses a statue of Our Lady of Guadalupe. "This is a shoeshine box which used to belong to my uncle, Refugio Leyba," she says. "He used to be a shoeshine boy around Santa Fe in the 1950s."

Felipe Trujillo grew up in the Rodarte area before moving to Taos. He was superintendent of the county schools before his retirement:

> *My mother was a very religious person. She always had an altar at the house. Our parents taught us to pray the rosary at an early age. We used to walk into the fields to celebrate the Feast of San Isidro. During El Mes de Maria (the month of May) we used to participate in the presentation of a play which was an old custom—it was 'El Ranchero y el Patron' held at my grandparents' private chapel in Rodarte. It is the story of San Isidro set in more modern times.*
>
> *My mother owned the first chapel in the community, near the old road. It was destroyed when the new road was built. People as a whole were very religious then. In the old days you always had to kneel down before older people to get a blessing. Many of the old ways have been forgotten now.*

Felipe Trujillo and son Roger, Talpa

Ralph Mondragón was born in Talpa in 1919 in the house next to where he and his wife Eliza now live:

> *I spent all my life practicing devotion from my parents and grandparents. By the time I was eight, ten years old, I was leading a Christian life. All young children were educated saying the rosary, and the Bible was very important. We always said our prayers before my parents' altar. We used to bring in fresh flowers beginning in the month of May.*

Eliza Mondragón, Ranchos de Taos

Pita Santistevan lives in Ranchos de Taos:

> *My parents had an altar. It was on top of the fireplace mantel. We lived across from the Ranchos Church. My mother was very devout; she belonged to the Sacred Heart League and was very devoted to San José Bendito de la Buena Muerte. Some years ago my husband was working for a contractor. He got a piece of steel in his eye. The doctor operated but then the redness wouldn't go away. The doctor told him if it doesn't go away, they were going to have to take out his eye. We came home from the doctor and said, "Let's start a novena to Our Lady of Lourdes," but I didn't have that one. So on Thursday evening we started a novena to Our Lady of Fatima. I had a small vial with water from the shrine at Lourdes and I put it in my husband's eye. The following Monday we went to the doctor and the redness was gone, so they didn't have to operate. This happened even though we hadn't finished our novena yet.*

Mela Garduño has a purple bedroom—everything from the walls to the bedspread and curtains:

> *I was born in Mora and we moved to Las Vegas when my dad died. I remember my grandmother had an altar in her house. My mother's was on top of the chest of drawers. She*

Santistevan family shrine, Ranchos de Taos

Mela Garduño, purple room shrine, Las Vegas

had St. Joseph, the Blessed Mother, Santo Niño, St. Anthony, and St. Jude. I've had my statue of Mother Cabrini for forty-five years. I bought it when I worked at a department store where they sold statues. Fifteen years ago I had cataracts and my eyesight was failing. I went to the eye doctor—they told me there was nothing they could do. I prayed to Mother Cabrini, St. Jude, and St. Teresa. When I went to another doctor, he suggested a corneal implant, which was done, and I've been able to see since then.

Mela sent us to her best friend's house, Pita Montoya, whose daughter is an insurance agent in Santa Fe:

Each saint has done a miracle for me, that's why I have them—they do miracles for me almost every day. When one of my daughters was thirteen, she came down with yellow jaundice. She was very sick. At the hospital I promised Saint Mother Cabrini I would go to the shrine in Denver if my daughter would get well. A few days later she was cured. We got married in 1936 during the depression. My husband started building the house in 1937; it was hard to get money. We almost lost our house. I prayed to St. Jude. My husband then got different jobs and finished building the house. My husband knew I gathered prayers so he built a box for me to keep all my novenas. I think of him every time I open it.

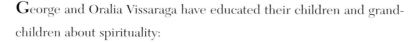

George and Oralia Vissaraga have educated their children and grand-children about spirituality:

> *My mother always had a devotional space at our home in Trampas. Our kids get blessed coming and going so that nothing will happen to them. We have six boys and fifteen grandchildren, and sometimes when it's too quiet in the house, I've seen the grandkids kneeling and praying near the altar and blessing themselves.*

Their altar is in a corner of the master bedroom. She attributes a major miracle to the saints on her altar:

> *In 1981 we used to own the gas station next to our house. One day we heard a loud explosion and my son saw the gas station go up in flames. He went running to help a man whose cigarette had set off the explosion. The man was killed and my son suffered burns to 80 percent of his body. We were told he would be in the hospital for three to six months. We prayed to the Blessed Mother and St. Joseph. Our son was out of the hospital in six weeks and on his way to recovery.*

Thelma Mares of Arroyo Hondo tells us her story:

> *My mom and grandma always recited the rosary daily. Mother was a big influence on me. In 1992 there was a bad*

Vissaraga family shrine, Peñasco

The statue of the saint who watched over the home and family received special treatment. It was hung with a leather thong from a nail on the wall. An arch-shaped *nicho* was sometimes cut in the adobe wall and then whitewashed. This housed a small altar with its candles and flowers. The term "*nicho*" was applied not only to the hollow in the wall but also to little chapel-like *nichos* constructed of carved wood or of tin and glass, as these materials became available. A statue of the Virgin would sit as comfortably in a painted wood *nicho* as she would in a hand-punched tin one. These *nichos* guarded the household saints from the dust and from dirt falling from the roof. These arched niches were decorated with lace curtains and paper flowers. A large family might install a high wooden *repisa*, or shelf, which could hold a number of saints.

The patronage of saints spread to all phases of territorial life. Occupations had their own special patrons. For instance, a farmer would pray to San Ysidro Labrador (Saint Isidore the Plowman) so that his crops would be increased; a rancher might pray to Santiago for the fertility of mares. On this subject, Thomas J. Steele writes:

> *In a society which had to rely on the most primitive sorts of folk medicine, the people often called on the saints for help in combating illness. In this broad field a number of the saints became very definitely specific to certain precise disorders or areas of the body. Thus St. Roch protects against troubles of the skin, plague and especially smallpox. St. Ros-*

alie of Palermo against the plague. St. Blaise guards against throat trouble, Saint Appolonia against toothache, St. Lucy against disease of the eye. St. Lawrence, who was burned to death, protects from burns, and St. Barbara guards persons against lightning. Thus are the most important threats to the health of the body fended off by the New Mexican saints.[5]

Every illness had its protector and every worry or anxiety its helper; even social stations and professions had their patron, practices alive today. The saints were resorted to in every life event, their names used on roads, towns, rivers, and winds. Every devout Catholic required a patron saint for his or her home altar. These patron saints were provided by *santeros* (saint-makers) who traveled from village to village selling homemade *santos* and taking orders for others. The altars were also decorated with lithographic prints of the saints, which were popularly available in the colony beginning in the early nineteenth century, framed in tin by the local tinsmith. These statues and paintings of patron saints were often carried from the church to private homes for the comfort of the sick and dying. They were accompanied by a group singing hymns and carrying lanterns or candles. Slivers from a wooden *santo* were often thrown out doors to quell a storm. The bases of statues were sometimes hollowed out and the wood burned to provide charcoal for Ash Wednesday blessings on the foreheads of the faithful.

Some saints even had their altars built outside. Shrines to Santa Ines (St. Agnes) are usually made of willows and roofed with boughs, as she is the patron saint of those who must live outdoors. A favorite of the people of rural and sheep-raising sections of New Mexico, part of the *alabado* (hymn of praise) in her honor goes as follows:

Aquí cantaremos	Praises here we sing
Este nombre santo,	to your Holy name
postrados a ti,	prostrate here before you
Santa Ines del Campo	Saint Agnes of hill and plain.[6]

An altar for San Ysidro Labrador was built on his feast day on May 15. On the eve of his day a procession of the farmers in the village would carry a statue of San Ysidro to the farthest farm in the valley. In anticipation of the arrival of the *santo*, the farmer would have built a small hut of willows and an altar decorated with fresh flowers. When the procession arrived, San Ysidro was placed in the miniature farm house, with candles lit on the altar table and bonfires surrounding the hut. Rosaries were prayed and songs sung into the late evening hours. At midnight food was served.

Early next morning on the feast day, San Ysidro is taken by procession to each farm, blessing the crops and lands of all as the procession winds its way down to the last farm. There they are greeted with a lunch consisting of roast mutton, bread, pies, and coffee. Returning to the village, San Ysidro is carried along the other side of the river, blessing the crops and lands on that side. One of the verses of the hymns sung to him is:

En tus bondades confiado	Confident in your goodness
Te pido de corazón	I ask you with my heart
Le mandes a mi sembrado	that you send my fields and/crops
favores y bendición.	favors and blessings.[7]

A *velorio de santo,* the night watch for a saint, is held when a special favor is requested or in fulfillment of a promise made for favors received. The image of a saint is placed on an altar in a special room of the house, and friends and neighbors are invited to a night of prayer, after which food is served at midnight. People kneel or sit on the mud floor surrounding the altar. The *resador* recites the rosary and special prayers, after which *alabados* are sung to the saints.

An altar traditionally is erected in a corner or against the wall by placing a table or bench covered with a sheet or embroidered linen cloth. The *santo* is then placed upon it and surrounded with tinsel and gay colored paper flowers. In the early days, *ramilletes* (paper roses) were made to decorate these home altars. They were dipped in melted wax and arranged into sprays. These paper decorations continued in use until the end of World War II. For hundreds of years these simple flowers have been made from whatever supplies were on hand: silk, straw, feathers, shells, wood, gourds, or paper. Since fresh flowers are generally available only from May through early fall, the use of these artificial altar flowers and evergreens is almost a necessity. As paper supplies became more common, New Mexican ladies became more proficient in this skill, crafting gorgeous flowers dipped in wax for the altar vases and to be used as bouquets and garlands. These were mixed with dried flowers and seedpods and continue to adorn the altars of the northern village churches, where they can still be seen in old vases next to the fresh flowers.

The use of candles on altars is a custom that dates back to pre-Christian times, not only for light but to signify the presence of God. Teresita Garcia Fountain writing at age eighty-eight recalled that candles were so scarce that her mother appointed her, whenever they had company at night, to sit near the candle and gather up the tallow as it melted and save it so that they could use it again. As nightfall approached, the family would kneel in front of their altar. By candlelight they would recite a rosary or novena. This discipline strengthened the cultural traditions of the family. After prayers were completed, the children and household servants knelt before the matriarch of the family to receive a blessing. This blessing was given by the parents each night before retiring or before embarking on a journey.

Every saint was treated as an equal to family members. These saints were rewarded with fresh flowers, candles, and new clothing. But many a saint has spent its days facing the wall, locked in a chest, or wrapped in a blanket because it has not granted the request of the devotee.

Today, as many urban and village homes continue to use the home altar as a special devotional space, the tradition of placing homemade or plaster saints on their altars still endures. This practice has been handed down from generation to generation. Store-bought candles are lit either on special occasions or on a daily basis. Fresh and dry bouquets of flowers are placed on the altar table, as are plastic flowers, rosaries, and statues.

The shrine in a Pueblo home typically holds both Catholic and traditional religious objects. A dance kilt covers the shelf, which holds a dance rattle made from a gourd and sacred corn alongside a statue of the patron saint of the pueblo, pictures of Catholic saints, votive candles, and a cross with rosary beads. The ear of corn is central to Pueblo life. It is given to dancers on the feast day and returned after the dance to ensure good fortune, good health, and goodwill.

Of the many public expressions of the ongoing faith among New Mexicans are the small devotional shrines that surround the Santuario de Chimayó in Northern New Mexico. Behind this famous healing place where each year tens of thousands of pilgrims converge, there is a park where outdoor masses are heard. This area has been in existence for many years, established to accommodate the overflow of pilgrims visiting Chimayó annually. Attached to the bars in front of each shrine are hundreds of small twig crosses made from the branches of nearby trees and held together by thin strips of bark. A bronze statue of Saint Francis sits within one of the stone grottos.

Throughout Chimayó there are many small grottos, evidence of the strong faith that has persisted since the santuario was built in 1816 by Don Bernardo Abeyta to serve the people of the surrounding community. Many legends are told relating to the finding of a black Cristo buried on the spot where the church was eventually built. After a statue of the Santo Niño de Atocha was acquired and placed in a shrine made from a nineteenth-century painted confessional next to the healing earth room, many people began to attribute their healing miracles to this Christ Child. The people of Northern New Mexico wholeheartedly believe that this Santo Niño was responsible for bringing back many local soldiers from World War II and Vietnam. Many miracles over the past fifty years have been attributed to this Niño. The walls of the shrine are lined with saints, pictures, handwritten prayers, and crutches, payment for miracles granted. Every year or so, all the articles left by grateful recipients of miracles are removed from the shrine and stored in a warehouse, only to be replaced by hundreds of others of the same nature.

The creation of altars and yard shrines combines a multitude of functions that include public declarations of faith and those that are most private. But it appears that all have the same theme running through them: personal, spiritual devotion. The tradition is commonly shared by older women: the *abuelas*, *tías*, and older cousins, but it appears that for whatever reason, whether it be tradition or a resurgence of spiritual values, the younger generation has begun to embrace and perpetuate the customs of their ancestors.

Helen Lee Gallegos, corner shrine, Santa Fe

Sweet Refuges/*Refugios dulces*
LUCY R. LIPPARD

"It's an ancient tradition, and you can't get away from it, wherever you go. My altarcito helps me to live."
—Doña Chole Pescina[1]

In the last five decades, the centuries-long isolation that bred a unique Northern New Mexican culture has drastically eroded. Yet history, memory, family, religion/spirituality, community, and local arts remain at the core of a rapidly changing culture. Despite the commodification of religious art in the Southwest, despite the avid curiosity of newcomers and new markets that have altered the arts, despite the lively academic debates taking place around ethnic identities, the basic beliefs hold firm. They hold lessons for those who question their significance. Nowhere are the personal/communal ramifications of such beliefs more evident than in the living shrines found in the parlors, workrooms, bedrooms, yards, and roadsides of Northern New Mexico.

Works of art with so solid a cultural base acquire layers of meaning as they survive the decades or centuries. There seems to be less of a rupture between past and contemporary art in native New Mexican culture (which includes Native or indigenous people and native or Spanish-speaking people) than elsewhere in the United States, yet even this continuity cannot heal the inevitable wounds sustained by such old cultures. Like the original Pueblo, Apache, and Ute inhabitants of this land, the descendants of the original Spanish-speaking families have adapted and reinvented the heritage of Northern New Mexico. They continue to do so, collaborating, sometimes uneasily, with the increasing number of Anglos who share their places.

Home shrines have a long and often contradictory history that goes back to household altars in prehistoric Europe, Greece, Rome, and Spain. The Old English word for altar meant "table of idols," and a similar nourishment for the soul, often laid out on lace tablecloths, continues today. Hearth altars also were common in the pre-Hispanic Americas. Although Roman Catholic dogma does not recognize home shrines, in early colonial Mexico they were encouraged as replacements for the indigenous shrines that were suspect for their connections to the

Personal shrine, Northern New Mexico

worship of earth power (eventually assimilated into Christianity, as testified to by the popular figure of Tonantzin/Guadalupe). The Jesuit author Thomas J. Steele writes that "Catholic sacramentalism demands to be understood in parallel with tribal, archaic religions, where differences of time, place, format, minister, and beneficiary are erased, so that the rite is identically the same event."[2]

Giving tangible form to theology within the household is a populist strategy, created in New Mexico in the eighteenth and nineteenth centuries by devout Catholics temporarily abandoned by the official church. Isolation even from Mexico produced a less ebullient, more somber and politically conservative style. The proliferation of home shrines was the result of the absence of clergy to attend to the people's spiritual needs, yet in parts of the Southwest the church used music and dance to draw people away from household worship and back into the churches. According to folklorist Kay Turner, home altars represent flexibility in contrast to the church's institutional rigidity. "Because it has been a predominantly women's tradition in a male-dominated Church," she writes, "and certainly because of its remarkable similarity (probably historically linked) to the pagan practice of maintaining 'house gods,' home altarmaking—a globally encountered folk tradition of the Roman Catholic faith, is denied any formal history by the institution which indirectly makes it possible."[3]

The makers and keepers of these shrines are almost always women, perhaps because the home is still the traditional female stronghold and the saints offer company during the day (or a life) when husband and children are absent. Perhaps it is because women are the creative arbiters of the indoors; or perhaps because without social equality, and with the high incidence of domestic violence and child abandonment common across cultures in this society, women need more help in dealing with their hard lives. Loss seems to be a major impetus for the creation of shrines.

The losses may be social as well as personal. Janet LeCompte has pointed out that unlike Anglo women in the East, who lost their economic power during the industrial revolution, New Mexican *hispanas*

Ida Martinez personal shrine, Arroyo Hondo

maintained a certain independence into the late nineteenth century, along with many legal rights already lost by other American women. The division of labor, she says, was more flexible in New Mexico, and class boundaries were less firm in a *mestizo* society.[4] Since then, poverty and lack of education in some sectors have taken their toll, often resulting in a self-effacing reticence within the broader Anglo-dominated society. The home altar is a refuge.

Turner, whose important work on women's altars is based on those of *Tejanas* rather than *Nuevo mexicanas* (and there are major differences), says altars help us understand the role played by women in facilitating relationships within the family-community context, and that the home altars demonstrate a generative principle that can also be applied to contemporary women's fine arts—a sense of connectedness and communally shared symbols: "Whether it is the labor of sustaining family ties, promoting the tenets of faith, or providing an embellished, beautiful environment, in the home the work of art is 'the work of kinship.'"[5] Women also act as mediators for the benefit of the whole family, especially those who have strayed, interceding with saints who in turn intercede with the upper echelons of the divine. Networking within the family is another facet, as shown by Chicana novelist Sandra Cisneros's irreverent account of waiting as a child outside the church for her grandmother:

> *There are so many prayers and promises and thanks-be-to-*
> *God to be given in the name of the husband and the sons*

Maxine Martinez family shrine, Valdez

and the only daughter who never attend mass. It doesn't matter. Like La Virgen de Guadalupe, the awful grandmother intercedes on their behalf. For the grandfather who hasn't believed in anything since the first PRI elections. For my father, El Periquin, so skinny he needs his sleep. For Auntie Light-skin, who only a few hours before was breakfasting on brain and goat tacos after dancing all night in the pink zone. For Uncle Fat-face, the blackest of the black sheep. . . . And Uncle Baby—You go for me Mama—God listens to you.[6]

The need for a daily spiritual presence is widespread today, in times that are in some ways as difficult for native New Mexicans as they were in the colonial period, but the longing for the sacred is national. More Americans belong to a church or a synagogue today (68 percent) than at the time of the American Revolution (17 percent), the Civil War (37 percent), or even in the family values–obsessed 1950s (around 50 percent). Sociologist Ronald Inglehart suggests that this burgeoning religiosity may be a legacy of the frontier mentality or simply a need for security.[7] The need for a predictable continuity, says Steele, leads to a fondness for "a set of visual 'commonplaces' where the verbal epithets of rhetorical commonplaces are replaced by the santos' visual attributes, their significant iconographic traits."[8] However, church attendance is not the only true indicator of the kind of strong faith that seems to inspire the *altarcitos*, and transforming the commonplace is an element of hope, a way of defining or imagining easier lives.

In an area (northern) and a state (New Mexico) so poor and so dependent on tourism, there is always a danger that artistic "authenticity" (a contested term in postmodern scholarship) will be sacrificed to economic considerations. But the home altars, if not the icons and objects upon them, are free of such pressures. The only "audience" aside from the powers being addressed is family and friends. The altar is the product of the maker's life. Untaught artisans are unburdened with the notion of artistic difficulty. Because theirs are private altars, personal devotions, they need conform to no one else's idea of what is

Artist Benjamin and Irene Lopez shrine, Española

proper, what is the right way to assemble them. The extraordinary variety found in these shrines results from the variety of spaces and personal tastes in which they are found. The makers' personalities are reflected in their modes of devotion. Few of the altars are even internally homogenous, and most are unself-consciously syncretic. Moreover, their religion often makes tangible to them areas where other artists fear to tread.

Each altar narrates a unique story of relationships, with its chosen saints, chosen photographs, chosen objects and mementoes that may

Teresa Sagel, weaving room shrine, Española

seem incongruous to anyone but the maker. Much as outsiders may admire the ensembles, no one but the maker really knows the deepest layers of meaning that lie in the placement, the addition and subtraction, the changes made in a home shrine. In fact, as in the process of looking at all art, the outside viewer brings to the altar her or his own needs and associations, which may or may not coincide with the maker's. If you knew enough about the maker and her circumstances, you could probably read her story in the altar. As it is, only clues are available to those unfamiliar with the intimate situations. The true meaning of the altarmaker's artistic creation, says Marie Romero Cash in this book, is "her need to express the love she has for her God and for herself. . . ." The emphasis on self-esteem and on relationship is significant.

The mother and child are of course the most ancient image of relationship. Mary is a "sweet refuge" (*refugio dulce*), part of a familial cosmology. The Virgin in one or more of her many guises is present on virtually all of the altars photographed for this book. "Why the mind-boggling multiplicity of Mary's titles?" asks Steele. "As Christian folklore has developed him, the devil is a shapeshifter, and we might conjecture that in order to keep up with him Mary has to assume a multitude of local names and iconographic forms. Or alternately, Mary . . . might need to localize and particularize herself in all the regions where the church wishes to be real."[9]

The roses found so often on home altars, paying homage with their fragrance, are the Virgin's flower and especially sacred to Guadalupe, who filled Juan Diego's *tilma* with roses in winter in the 1531 miracle. The altar blossoms may be fresh or made of paper (the traditional *ramilletes* that date from the early eighteenth century) or of plastic. (Those who disdain plastic flowers as "kitsch" disregard this lineage.) Lilies appear on the altars around Easter. Along with candles (representing light and the spirit in so many cultures) and birds (also messengers between heaven and earth), mirrors are common in or near home shrines. The *santo*, says Steele, "is very much like a mirror [mak-

Lopez family shrine, Española

ing] possible a two-way visual communication between earth and heaven, between heaven and earth."[10]

For Santa Feans, La Conquistadora, also known as the Virgin of the Assumption and Our Lady of the Rosary (Rosario), is supposedly the favored Marian devotion. She is the central figure of the late summer Fiesta celebrating Don Diego de Vargas's mythically "bloodless reconquest" of New Mexico after the Pueblo Revolt of 1680–93. But it is Guadalupe who is found far more often on these home altars. According to Ronald Grimes, La Conquistadora was favored by the rich and powerful; Guadalupe in her Mexican devotion is the patron saint of

Candido and Crucita Ortiz, family shrine, Las Vegas

the poor, associated with indigenous heritage and with the "secular period" of New Mexico history (1790–1850). She is even considered by some to be "anti-Spanish." Grimes finds two Guadalupes in New Mexico—the Mexican militant symbol and a more conservative "Spanish" local figure.[11] The two meanings may be conflated on these altars, or the second may have conceptually subsumed the first despite the identical imagery.

Altars, like prayers, are mediators, collaborative forms crafted to reach across the abyss between known and unknown. The home altars—some spare and ascetic, some tidy and symmetrical, some ornate, some relatively seamless, others joyful accumulations of anything that comes to hand that seems to have meaning—modestly echo the great religious art of European cathedrals and the remarkable works of elegant and naive arts, the *retablos, reredos,* and *santos* found in the little rural churches in Chimayó or Las Trampas or at Laguna, Acoma, or Zuni pueblos. A common need for something that can be seen, touched, and felt reaches even those raised in abstracted Protestantism or iconoclastic Judaism and Islam. Despite the museumist convention that "real art" must be separated from "crafts" and "folk art," these marvelous conglomerations of spiritual and popular culture, of imposed and original conceptions, are certainly works of art (expressions of culture), although few were intended as such. Some shrines are far less inventive and brilliantly creative than others, which goes for "high art" of all kinds, too, but others clearly spring from that reservoir of passion and grace that is the source of all good art of any style or culture.

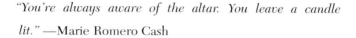

"You're always aware of the altar. You leave a candle lit." —Marie Romero Cash

Institutional religion and home religion (*religion casera*), personal and communal life, coexist in the *altarcitos de casa*. The language and vocabulary of the shrines have developed within local culture and complex family networks. They are tucked into familiar interiors like microcosms of the little churches in the mountainous landscape. Where a church creates its own separate spiritual atmosphere, an altar is embraced by and intertwined with daily life. Its flickering candles may be quiet participants in family events or the altar may be the center of someone's private space in a bedroom or office. The shrines in this book are found on tables, dressers, iceboxes, cabinets, mantels, perched on the back of a couch, on a stereo, or on a television (which has its own patron saint—Santa Clara). They also live in *nichos* of all kinds, traditional containers that provide an aura of protection or sacred space around them. Armoires and ironing boards, stuffed animals and cosmetics, American flags and fresh flowers, working tools and secular tchotchkes keep them company.

The accretions on and around a home shrine are inclusive, embracing many aspects of daily life by means of what artists call "found objects." In the photograph of Ray Herrera's home, a tower pointing toward heaven is based on a structurally beautiful old icebox surmounted by a wooden *nicho* with the Holy Family on which is mounted a candle in an aluminum take-out container, all triumphantly

Artist Lydia Garcia's personal shrine, Ranchos de Taos

Ray Herrera, workshop shrine, Santa Fe

José and Guillerma Romero shrine, Talpa

Maria Lopez shrine, Albuquerque

crowned by a framed Virgin of Guadalupe. At the sides are St. Joseph and child, a Spanish Market poster, some new wooden shutters waiting to be installed, and an oxen yoke. The ensemble is casual, and the shrine seamlessly incorporates its surroundings.

Maria Lopez's polished, ordered, and elegant altar in Albuquerque also utilizes found objects: an antique clock case to hold a baroque Virgin, an elaborate gold frame that now holds two more old sculptured Virgins on rounded shelves. Votive candles are doubled by their reflections in the polished surface and brass candelabra. The carefully composed effect of these reds and golds is one of opulence.

The saints displayed on home altars may be rare antiques, beautifully rendered old *santos* of New Mexican Catholic tradition, more recent offspring of that heritage, or they may be nineteenth- and twentieth-century plaster, mass-produced and inexpensive. Their esthetic or monetary value is irrelevant to their efficacy and to the owner's piety. While elaborate and beautiful saints and altars are much appreciated, the smallest, plainest saints are just as powerful and loved. "The altar tradition is a sign of *being* Catholic, not just being Catholic for appearances' sake," says Cash, "but being Catholic from the heart. These altars project the faith of the believer into the heavenly realm, which they know exists but to which they have no access other than by the daily prayers said to the saints on their altars."

What, then, are we to make of altars by Anglos and non-Catholics? The *hispano* altars are patently *at home* in a climate of faith and devotion intersecting with everyday life in ways totally unfamiliar to Protestants, whose religion Turner calls "truly patriarchal . . . in its complete denial of feminine imagery and power."[12] This may be why the "gringo altar," lately popular in New Mexico, can be visually striking but usually seems more decorative than functional. Beauty itself can be deeply felt, of course, but the depth of devotion in the local home altars is sometimes expressed by the very lack of overt esthetic attention. The beauty seems to come from a different source. My own home has several icons of Catholicism, although I am basically a pan-

Polly Brown chapel shrine, Jacona

Jim Fickey and Gary Grimm shrine, Galisteo

theist. An elderly native New Mexican visitor, about to undergo cataract surgery, commented on seeing my plaster Santa Lucia that she was just completing a novena to the patron saint of eyesight (also a good name saint for an art critic). A local *curandero* remarked that the conglomeration of objects and family pictures in my house looked like his workplace. Neighbors have eyed my Haitian crucifix, made from an old oil drum, and wondered why I don't show up in church. While my respect for the meanings of these objects is part of my enjoyment of their beauty, the personal religious dimension is absent.

Jack Green, shrine to son Noah, Santa Fe

"And so our dead ones are within us and none is left behind." —Mercedes Sosa[13]

The introduction of ritual into the domestic sphere also means the introduction of the family into religious practice. The Holy Family and the saints share their altars with old and new family photographs. William Beezeley suggests that the shrines can be seen as family albums or visual family trees.[14] Familial lineage and genealogical links become connected with those of the heavenly family and the hierarchal church during family-based practice. The saints are themselves like family members. They are talked to, dressed up, punished, and rewarded. They may indeed have been a presence for generations, sharing the altarmaker's whole life. The artists arrange and rearrange their displays depending on what is happening in their lives. The shrines grow organically, reflecting daily events, catastrophes, losses, romantic complications, illnesses, births, deaths, and relatively minor disturbances and celebrations. Some of the altarmakers are *santeras* in their own right or have participated in the artforms taught and exchanged within the family, as is the case with the accomplished (and creatively innovative) *santera* Marie Romero Cash, and her parents, nationally honored tinsmiths Emilio and Senaida Romero. Her shrine currently concentrates on her brother, the well-known tinworker Robert Romero, and on her father, Emilio, who died recently, but its direction, too, will change.

If religion seems less important to younger generations of New Mexican Catholics, its integral part in the network of family, community, and place is the thread that at least tenuously continues to connnect all three. The *bultos, retablos*, plaster figures, chromolithographs, and velvet paintings found on shrines along with family pictures and mementoes are the agents of this continuity. As Ramon Gutierrez has said of Mexican home altars, "When visitors or residents of the household stand before these altars in simple acts of prayer, reflection, and meditation, they place themselves and their family in that grander cosmic scheme of memory and history."[15]

Gloria Quinto, in Ranchos de Taos, New Mexico, maintains three shrines, one dedicated to her farmer-grandfather. She says, "I talk to the saints and it calms me down." California artist and writer Amalia Mesa-Bains writes that as an art form, the shrine, with its ceremonial esthetic, "springs from the experience of the emigre, the curandero and the lost devotional. In the experience of separation and expatriation lingers the sense of loss."[16] Making a shrine is part of the healing process. Elena Avila, a professional *curandera* living in Rio Rancho, has an altar facing east where the sun comes up. It is a community altar, with a candle lit for everyone who comes to her for healing. Avila's altar also asserts her *mestizaje*, or Indo-hispano, heritage. A pre-Columbian mask with a feather headdress, an Aztec warrior figurine, eagle feathers, and Plains Indian beadwork coexist with the Virgin of Guadalupe and other Catholic images.

Juan Ortega family shrine, Llano Largo

Quinto family shrine, Ranchos de Taos

"What the mestizaje of the Americas has created is that now the other is also within us." —Victor Hernandez Cruz[17]

New combinations of ancient images and beliefs are constantly evolving or revolving through the mirrored doors of cultural negotiation. Despite the urgent social issues of racism and cultural bias that persist in New Mexico, I do not believe that the ubiquity of Guadalupe (*La Morena*, the Indo-Hispanic icon who is nevertheless popularly pictured as white with Mediterranean features) and the importance of the black Christ of Esquipulas worshiped at Chimayó mean that these figures have any racial significance. The frequent appearance of the black male icon San Martin de Porres on the photographed altars is ignored in the literature.[18] Although New Mexicans are "racially" Indo-Hispanic (probably a quarter to a third American Indian) but culturally Hispanic/Iberian, in historic New Mexico, according to Steele, "there was no way of 'living culturally and religiously mestizo.' A given family either spoke Spanish as their mother tongue and worshiped in the Catholic-Penitente fashion, or they spoke an Indian language as their mother tongue, lived in a pueblo or with a nomadic tribe, and participated in the Pueblo dances (along with being Catholic) or in the Navajo or other Indian rituals." The current preoccupation of those New Mexicans who see themselves as "Spanish" and do not identify politically with Chicanos or culturally with more recent Mexican immigrants dates from the 1910s and 1920s, around the same

Elena Avila in front of healing room shrine, Rio Rancho

Outdoor shrine, Santuario de Chimayó

Teresa Martinez, deceased mother Cecelia's shrine,
Picurís Pueblo

time that the term "Spanish Colonial" came into fashion and the colonial arts were revived for upper-class and Anglo consumption.[19]

Fragmentation and accumulation, layering and repetition, are the underlying collage esthetics of the shrines, as they are of women's work, women's lives, and (more self-consciously) feminist art in the 1970s. They are classic examples of collage, bricolage, or liturgical patchwork, random clusters with an organic logic testifying to the power of repetition and imitation. "As a general principle," writes Steele, "a ritual article or action is more powerful (first) the more authentically it imitates its prototype and (second) the more holy and powerful that prototype is. . . . The santero can assume that he is making his santo right if he is making it 'the way it's always been done,' the way the tradition indicates."[20] Yet in the shrines, such repetition of parts provides the rhythm of the always new whole.

Although fragmentation is the natural style of these altars, it is used to reveal and heal dissonance between past and present, between expectations and reality. Eclectic accretions of recontextualized *recuerdos* are placed in what might be called "bilingual" (double-tongued) or "polyvocal" (many-voiced) arrangements. Because placement is the tool with which new wholes are created from fragments, the specific juxtaposition and superposition of images and objects are particularly fascinating. It would be ludicrous to analyze the altars from a formal viewpoint, not only because they are constantly changing but because the intention is not to please or provoke others but to facilitate an inti-

Bersaba Lujan, Ropero shrine, Rio Lucio

of backgrounds—perhaps because of the implication of inclusiveness and acceptance as opposed to elitist exclusion and rejection. In Santa Fe each year around Halloween, there is a multigallery "shrine show" initiated by the community of artists who have lived here for twenty years or more and drawing newcomers.

In the Northern New Mexico landscape, the saints are everywhere, recalled by place names, churches, schools, and pueblos. In an attempt to focus this book, related shrines in cemeteries, churches, roadside *descansos*, and memorial sites have been omitted. The only outdoor works included here are private altars in yards, along roadsides, and those made by unidentified makers that are found in the wilderness, some of which also perform memorial functions. Such mementoes are ubiquitous. Whenever I drive to town, I pass a sandstone marker to Lucy Tafoya, who died at a nearby intersection. In my own village, there is a little shrine remembering Tobias Anaya, a well-known local vernacular artist, and nearby, a cross and painting made by his brother Tony that marks the site of the village's oldest church. A few houses away is a lovingly rendered miniature replica of the present village church overlooking the real Nuestra Señora de los Remedios, made by their brother-in-law Manuel Anaya.

Outsiders travel to and often settle in New Mexico because of what almost everyone takes for granted as the inherent "spirituality" of the landscape. New Mexican natives watch, sometimes helplessly,

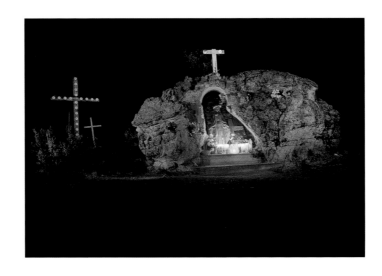

Outdoor shrine to the Virgin, Abiquiu

Outdoor shrine, Gaby Martinez family, Agua Fria Street

Santo Niño in roadside cave shrine, Ribera

sometimes admiringly, sometimes angrily, as that landscape changes, an ironic consequence of this perception. More poignant to many new-comers than the organized Roman Catholic religion are visible connections, through religious symbolism, to the land, to history, and to the "spirit" of the place, which unfortunately has been so commercially and "spiritually" exploited that the phrase is losing its meaning. Time, like space, is a major element in the home altars, which often feature within their "timeless" imagery ephemeral elements such as fresh flowers, plants, and candles reflecting the transitory quality of life itself. It makes sense, especially to those coming out of an oral tradition and a down-to-earth agricultural tradition, to pray to someone who is there, who shares one's own space, rather than to an abstraction.

> *Prayers and faith weave through our relatives' words like*
> *floral scents weave through the garden.* —Pat Mora.[24]

Outdoor shrines had a different meaning when people lived closer to nature. Pueblo peoples marked sacred places with extraordinary panels of rock art or with stone shrines, rock piles, circles, or crescents on sites that command exquisite views and also echo their surroundings. Later, *hispano* farmers, shepherds, and ranchers carved large crosses while watching their stock. Near Native petroglyphs—especially those of snakes—shepherds carved small crosses to ward off

Rock shrine to the Virgin, Abiquiu

Desert shrine, Cerrillos

the pagan evil. They inscribed their names or initials to proclaim their presence in those vast spaces, as Native people before them had asserted their prayers with handprints. The home altar itself follows the seasons through religious celebrations, not unlike rural agricultural work.

Today, however, the spirits of place have given way to the Virgin and her son. The ancient cairns and rock shrines have evolved into grottos in yards and at roadsides. Unexpected objects (marbles, stuffed animals) find their way into these outdoor altars as they do indoors. Though small in scale, the stone roadside shrines are often striking in their relationship to their places, which may aggrandize or miniaturize the humanmade additions. Near Ribera, for example, the shrine's dome echoes the round hills where it is set. Roadside and yard shrines, or *nichos* in walls facing the street, tell the world that a devout family lives here. Some, like Shirley Ardeuleta's, are neatly manicured and well kept. The figures are always embraced in curves, from natural rock to a half-buried bathtub to an arch of artificial flowers. Some retain a wilder aspect, like the Santo Niño at Ribera, doubly framed by an arch of white flowers and a natural rock alcove, or the virgin at Cerrillos, set in a natural sandstone grotto. Some are particularly dramatic at night when their points of electric lighting reflect the stars. Others, like Ray Herrera's miniature stone and wood church (see page 11), set into a hillside row of houses as though it were simply one of them, are urban landmarks. Altars may be placed in a home's windows facing out to the

Joe Ortiz family shrine, Las Vegas

Roadside shrine, Peñasco

Roadside shrine with marbles, Picurís/Embudo highway

street, the sill becoming a miniature stage backed by a curtain or venetian blind. Sometimes altars are even found in storefronts, where they take on a more secular guise, as in the Las Vegas window featuring Nancy Reagan sitting on Mr. T's lap. Each of these, in its own way, becomes public art.

Like the indoor shrines, those outdoors are temporal. They change and disappear and reappear depending on the whims, abilities, lives, and lifespans of their caretakers. Mobility is in a sense built into the process. As Romero Cash points out, the first Catholic shrines in New Spain were portable, carried in by the exploring priests and soldiers. Later the mission priests traveled far and wide to their *visitas*, while wealthier landowners erected their own *capillas* and *oratorios*. The early *santeros* were itinerant, carving at home and then setting out to sell their wares in faraway villages. Mobility was the counterpoint and often the motivation for the traditional *religion casera* and *altarcitos de casa*. Common religion bound people together and offered a certain emotional security in lonely and dangerous places. Throughout the twentieth century, even the most devoted family men in the northern villages have been forced to travel to other counties or states to find work, and the saints presiding over the home shrines heard prayers for their safe return, as well as those for the protection and well-being of family members in the military service. Lowriders such as Chimayó's renowned Lolo Martinez or Nicolas Herrera in El Rito take their shrines with them on the road, on the dashboards or painted in elabo-

Daniel Martinez family yard shrine, Ribera

Storefront window shrine, Bridge Street, Las Vegas

Cecelio and Rita Gurule, yard shrine, Las Vegas

Nicolas Herrera, family shrine, El Rito

rate detail on the outside of their cars. To commemorate another kind of absence, a *pano* (pen drawing on a handkerchief) may have been made by a son in prison, and religious tattoos might be seen as the ultimate in personal, and mobile, shrines.

This book is the result of a noteworthy collaboration between a native New Mexican *santera* who comes from a family of traditional artists and a Santa Fe photographer born in Salzburg, Austria, who has a similar background. Siegfried Halus's father was a liturgical sculptor who worked on European and then American churches and synagogues. Halus himself, raised Roman Catholic and Romanian Orthodox, worked as his father's apprentice and has been a restorer as well as a sculptor, teacher, and avant-garde photographer. Admiring the New Mexican artists' tenacious retention of a stylistic moment from their distant past and the way it is absorbed into home altars, he brings to his visual representations a comprehension of religion, art, and exile. Halus's subtle and unpretentious photographs of the shrines are artful fusions of self-effacement (he has made it clear that this book is about the altarmakers, not about his work) and a skilled artist's confident eye. His rapport with the old artisans, and the empathy he feels with those making these shrines, made him acutely sensitive to the dangers of reducing these deeply felt personal places to the role of mere curiosities.

Such work is important because it asserts the importance of this particular neglected art and also engenders respect for the Spanish-

Martinez family shrine, Ribera

90   speaking Catholic culture that produces it. The cross-cultural need for mutual respect is demonstrated daily in Northern New Mexico. If fiercely defended cultural pride is a shield against "that worst of all disasters, a people's loss of confidence in their way of life,"[25] the living shrines, in their gentle way, perform the same function.

Wanda Dawley, fireplace shrine, Galisteo

Sheila Keefe, Nambé

Quinto family shrine, Taos

Carmen Velarde personal shrine, Ranchos de Taos

Lydia Mondragon, Llano Quemado

Fireplace shrine, Las Vegas

Day of the Dead Shrine, Grant and Patricia LaFarge,
Santa Fe

Outdoor shrine, Santuario de Chimayo

Trujillo family shrine, Talpa

Outdoor shrine, in memory of Ramon Lopez's mother,
Santa Fe

Eugenia Parry, fireplace shrine, Santa Fe

Carmelita and Susie Romero, Truchas

Connie Hernandez, 1930s shrine, old Santa Fe

Julia T. Rodriguez, bedroom shrine, Santa Fe

Window shrine, Gurule Home, Santa Fe

Northern New Mexico shrine

Dresser top shrine, Las Vegas

My aunt Brigida Gabaldon (deceased),
Ninita Street shrine, Santa Fe

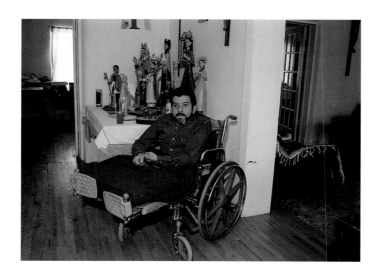

Santero Luisito Lujan, Nambé

Pacheco family shrine, Española

*Candido and Crucita Ortiz, with son Benny,
Grandson José and daughter-in-law Julia in front of
bathtub shrine, Las Vegas*

Kepler family outdoor shrine, Santa Fe

Shirley Archuleta, outdoor shrine, Dixon

Shrine to the Virgin, Rancho de Santa María de la Paz,
Peña Blanca, María Margarita Maranon, Galisteo

Notes

Altares de la Gente

1. Eleanor B. Adams and Fray Angelico Chávez, eds. and trans., *The Missions of New Mexico 1776: A Description by Fray Francisco Atanasio Dominguez, with Other Contemporary Documents* (Albuquerque: University of New Mexico Press, 1956), 90.

2. Marta Weigle and Peter White, *The Lore of New Mexico* (Albuquerque: University of New Mexico Press, 1988), 162–3.

3. W. W. H. Davis, *El Gringo, or New Mexico and Her People* (New York: Harper and Bros., 1857), 40.

4. W. H. Emory with J. W. Abert, "Notes of a Military Reconnaissance from Fort Leavenworth, in Missouri to San Diego, in California . . . ," 1846–47, Report of the Secretary of War, 30th Congress, Executive Document 41, Washington, 1848.

5. Thomas J. Steele, *Santos and Saints: The Religious Folk Art of Hispanic New Mexico* (Santa Fe: Ancient City Press, 1994), 134.

6. Lorin W. Brown, *Hispano Folklife of New Mexico: The Lorin W. Brown Federal Writers' Project Manuscripts* (Albuqerque: University of New Mexico Press, 1978), 157–58.

7. Ibid., 187.

1. Doña Chole Pescina, a Tejana quoted by Kay Turner in "The Art of Devotion: Texas-Mexican Expressions of Faith," in Inverna Lockpez, ed., *Chicano Expressions.* (New York: Intar Latin American Gallery, 1986), 41.

2. Thomas J. Steele, *Santos and Saints: The Religious Folk Art of Hispanic New Mexico* (Santa Fe: Ancient City Press, 1994), 100.

3. Kay Turner, "Women's Home Altars: A Creative Expression of Power as Relationship," manuscript for paper delivered at a meeting of the American Folk Lore Society, 1979.

4. Janet LeCompte, "The Independent Women of Hispanic New Mexico, 1821–1846," *Western Historical Quarterly*, January 1981.

5. Kay Turner and Pat Jasper, "Domains of Expression: La Casa, La Calle, y La Esquina," in *Arte Entre Nosotros/Art Among Us* (San Antonio: San Antonio Museum of Art, 1986), 23.

6. Sandra Cisneros, "Mericans," in Patricio Chavez, Madeleine Grynsztejn, and Kathryn Kanjo, eds., *La Frontera/The Border* (San Diego: Centro Cultural de la Raza and Museum of Contemporary Art, 1993), 125.

7. Ronald Inglehart, quoted in Richard Morin, "Keeping the Faith," *Washington Post National Weekend Edition* (January 12, 1998): 37.

8. Steele, *Santos and Saints,* 108.

9. Ibid., 56.

10. Ibid., 85.

11. Ronald L. Grimes, *Symbol and Conquest : Public Ritual and Drama in Santa Fe, New Mexico* (Ithaca: Cornell University Press, 1976), 242. Jacqueline Dunnington, in *Viva Guadalupe! The Virgin in New Mexican Popular Art* (Santa Fe: Museum of New Mexico Press, 1997), 18–19, points out that the Spanish encountered Guadalupe while in exile in El Paso/Juárez and that de Vargas gave thanks to her for his safe return to Santa Fe, thus opening the door to the devotion in this area. Anthropologist Phyllis Passariello suggests a trickster identity for Guadalupe, which seems appropriate to all of her interpretations (manuscript for paper presented at SSA meeting, 1996).

12. Turner, "Women's Home Altars."

13. Mercedes Sosa, quoted in Susana Torruella Leval, ed., *Reaffirming Spirituality* (New York: El Museo del Barrio, 1995), 45. This interesting exhibition gathered a number of Latino artists to respond to works in the museum's collection, many of which are santos and religious works.

14. In Dana Salvo, *Home Altars of Mexico*, Albuquerque: University of New Mexico Press, 1997), 100, 102. Texts by Ramon A. Gutierrez, Salvatore Scalora, William H. Beezley and Amalia Mesa-Bains.

15. Ramon A. Gutierrez in Ibid, 18.

16. Amalia Mesa-Bains, in Amalia Mesa-Bains and Robert Gaylor, eds., *Ceremony of Memory: New Expressions in Spirituality Among Contemporaruy Hispanic Artists* (Santa Fe: Center for Contemporary Arts, 1989–90), 7.

17. Victor Hernandez Cruz (a New York poet who is a product of the Puerto Rican diaspora), in the newsletter *Poetry Project* (Fall 1997): 5.

120   18. I became acquainted with San Martin de Porres while living in New York; he carries a broom and is beloved of Puerto Rican Catholics there.

19. Steele, *Santos and Saints,* 68–69

20. Ibid., 82

21. Turner, "Women's Home Altars"

22. Victor Zamudio-Taylor, in Mesa-Bains and Gaylor, *Ceremony of Memory*, 15.

23. Quoted in Leval, *Reaffirming Spirituality*, 24, 49.

24. Pat Mora, *House of Houses* (Boston: Beacon Press, 1997), 16.

25. Steele, *Santos and Saints*, 114.